My Spiritual Sister

By

Lauren Walker

Published by Lauren Walker.
Made in USA.

2017

Cover credit: Brad Gantt.
Interior Design credit: Brandon Telg.

ISBN-13: 978-1978006874
ISBN-10: 197800687X

Email: myspiritualsister2015@gmail.com

Contents

Acknowledgements

There were many layers of events that occurred before my words ended up on paper and therefore, many layers of individuals to acknowledge. From the moment of my sister's passing, I want to thank each person who gave up their personal time to show concern for my family, each person who donated to Chloe's GoFundMe, each person who attended the 5K race in her memory, each person who shared with me any time they had a spiritual "Chloe moment" and each person that attended her Celebration of Life ceremony. An especially big thanks goes out to those who still ask about Chloe today.

Thank you to my family for reacting with pride when I shared my dream of being an author.

Thank you to the dear friends surrounding me that helped me through the writing process including jotting down memories, talking through the sequence of the chapters, self-editing, self-publishing, and proofreading.

Thank you to Shands Rehabilitation Hospital in Gainesville, Florida for allowing me the time I needed to be with family on such short notice, and for being the local family I have so greatly cherished in my life.

Thank you to Brandon Telg for offering out of the goodness of his heart to be my mentor and internal formatter, whether or not you truly knew what you were getting into.

To
My Little Buddy

Chapter One

MY future children will not have an aunt...unless I marry someone with a sister. Where is her body at this very moment? Will I have to ID her? Is it in a hospital? Was someone with her? I will never hear her laugh again. This is what it feels like to be an only child...How am I going to deal with Mom and Dad on my own? Was she scared? Why didn't she call me? My duties as an older sister to keep my little sister safe, have been failed. What were her last words? Her last thoughts? Her last sights and sounds? Her heart actually had a last beat, her lungs actually had a last breath... Who will I dance with ever again? Who will understand my sense of humor? What is going to happen to her pets? How much does dying cost? Where are her belongings? Was she drinking? How long have they known before they called me? Who witnessed this? This is the longest drive of my life even though it is only two hours to Orlando, FL from Gainesville, FL...What is my mom going to look like when I see her for the first time after she has lost her youngest daughter? Who should I call, in what order, to notify? What about all the things we are going to have to take care of such as her new apartment, her credit cards, her bills, her school. I don't have a sister anymore...I don't have a sibling, at all, anymore...

It seems as though this list of thoughts could fill up an entire day's worth of thinking. They happened in less than five minutes. My mind was on overdrive, like an old-time movie reel clicking forward with no one to operate the "pause," or "stop," buttons.

These were the first few moments after I was notified that my little sister, Chloe, had died in a car accident. These were the first few moments after I heard a part of my mother's heart leave her chest forever, as she cried, "my baby, my baby!", over the phone. And then I knew, without a single detail being shared...that Chloe was gone.

Packing a suitcase for any trip is bad enough. Planning for the weather, your activities, your length of stay, your personal belongings. I stared at my empty suitcase, as it filled with my salty tears, all I could logically conclude was that I would need to pack a black dress...my mind could not execute any higher functions than that at this very moment. So I placed my black dress and black shoes in the suitcase and began the unknown journey of grieving.

Chapter Two

A sherrif came to my home, where my family, my sister's boyfriend, and his family, stood, to hear that Chloe's car went 18 feet underwater into a retention pond. A pond that I used to drive by every day. Some "pond" for 18 feet deep, it should be considered a lake. This is no shallow, serene, surface with lily pads and ducks floating. It mysteriously engulfed a 4-door car along with my sister's beautiful body and soul. I couldn't explain the rage I had towards the Sheriff, who was a complete stranger to Chloe but had the privilege to know more information about her death than I did. He had come to help us, and I envied him. It was illogical as many things would turn out to be in the next two years without Chloe.

Tears, red cheeks, mucus, and sweat filled the room, as no one knew what to do next, except missing her desperately.

The Sheriff pulled me away to give me a bag of her belongings that they had pulled from the car. Chloe's glittery, high heel shoes, that only she could pull off wearing. Her soaking wet wallet, credit cards, and money, her purse, and clothes. This is fake, right? I immediately started laying everything out to dry, separating each and every rewards card and dollar bill, as if drying these things out would give me a clue as to what happened, or where she was, or maybe even bring her back...

It was only a nauseating two hours before news teams showed up at our door, what could they have possibly expected from a family whose hearts have been ripped out, whose minds can't focus, or whose bodies are even functioning. We weren't eating, we weren't sleeping, we were in shock. But it would make for a good news story.

As the news spread, neighbors, friends, and family came by. I hated that every time I got a new hug, I would start crying all over again. Then catch my breath, and then someone else would walk through the door, and it would start all over again. I had never been so thankful for the "decline," feature on my cell phone, as the calls came rolling in. I had never been so thankful for the ability to send a text message because it meant that I did not have to try and force words without tears, nor hear other's emotional voices over the phone. The statements "how are you doing,?" and "I am sorry for your loss," never seemed more idiotic, but on the flip side, if people didn't say anything, they would look heartless. There needs to be a better greeting made up when you approach someone who has just experienced death.

My eyes were swollen, shiny, my nose raw, my stomach in knots, and my chest so tight. Despite my physical pain, I knew I had to be the grounded one, the one to ask, realistically, what do we do next? Is there a to-do list for dealing with a deceased loved one? A "Death for Dummies," book?

Chapter Three

AT this point in my twenty-five years of life, the medical examiner's office was something that only existed on the Discovery Health Channel. I had never laid eyes on a medical examiner building, although there is one in each district. It played no role in my life, until I had to wrap my head around the fact that my little sister was now in that building, and it did exist. Do they actually use the cold metal tables, and white bags, and "Y" cut incisions? I felt a similar frustration towards the medical examiner as I had earlier towards the Sheriff, I was envious that I had not been able to touch or feel my sister since I had seen her last, and never will again, but yet a stranger will be able to know her intimately, inside and out after the autopsy. They will be able to see and feel the tattoo on her hip; the same tattoo that I shared with her, "...and then the stars didn't seem so far away," but yet I will only be able to see it in pictures and memories.

I had to be the one that called the medical examiners office because my mother, understandably, could not fathom it. The person on the other end of the phone probably thought they were speaking to a brick wall since all I could do was shake my head and say "okay." I was told that Chloe's cause of death was drowning and that her body would be ready to be transferred to the funeral home of our choosing soon. They asked if we had decided on a viewing versus closed casket for the service, in order to relay the condition of her body. I guess not everyone after death is appropriate for a viewing based on injuries. A viewing? I haven't even swallowed the idea of any type of end-of-life service. I didn't even know if Chloe wanted to be cremated or buried. There was no will. Wait, her body now has to be transported somewhere? Like in a hearse? There is going to be people driving on the street next to the vehicle that contains my beautiful sister's body and they are not even going to think once, let alone twice that it is her, or know what happened to her, MY sister. Once again, this rapid envy came over me. There were only precious hours left where my sister would have her physical form before it became remains, and strangers were able to spend that time next to her on the roadways instead of me.

It was heart-shredding to have to approach my mother and tell her that we needed to begin planning. We needed to pull it together enough to begin the process of Chloe's memorial service. We researched the different funeral homes in our area and began asking questions and making phone calls. I wish I could, but I will never forget sitting at a table in a private room when I was asked what kind of wood that we wanted Chloe's casket to be made of. Each question that I was faced with shocked and baffled me, and I thought I could not be taken aback anymore until I was asked what outfit Chloe would be dressed in for her viewing.

My mother, sister, and I had many fond memories of shopping together. "Back-to-school," seasons were a time when the majority of our hours awake were in malls and department stores. My mother used this as an outlet to show her love and interest in us, and Chloe and I enjoyed being some of the best-dressed at school. What girls wouldn't? I can't say it was a healthy habit, but it was one that the three of us shared. My mother and I had to imagine shopping without Chloe, instead, for Chloe. We stood in the middle of Kohl's as empty shells, scared to even say out loud what our opinions should be of Chloe's last outfit. Do you pick something she would have worn normally? Do you pick something angelic? With color? White for heaven? Black for death? "It needs to be something large or easy to get on," stated the funeral home director...in order to get over a body that has gone through embalming. It made us sick. We were on our knees, hidden by the metal racks of clothing on all four sides of us, crying into clothes, not caring if we were ruining them.

We went with innocent and angelic...her favorite colored-shirt (yellow) and a white cardigan, an enchanting cross-necklace, and dress pants. Would she have picked it herself? No. But this is how my Mom wanted her image as her "baby girl," to be preserved forever. Again, the bewilderedness continued as I was consulted on how my sister's hair should be styled and how her makeup should be done. I knew no matter what, a funeral home director was not going to do justice to someone's hair who walked out of the front door looking like a movie star each morning. We went with soft curls, light lipstick, and light mascara. Again, angelic.

The songs to play, the catering company to choose, the decorations to pick, the flowers to order, how to spread the word, it was consuming. It was parasitic, there was nothing left in me to give.

Approximately two weeks prior to Chloe's accident, she called me one night while driving in her car, after we had been playing days of phone tag, dodging busy schedules. She asked me if I had ever heard the song "See You Again." It was playing dimly in the background as she spoke. It was a new song on the radio at this point, but I had heard it enough to recognize it. She told me that she had been reflecting amongst our attempts to reach each other, and told me that she was so thankful that she got me as her older sister, that she could have been born into any family, but she got one with me in it. She felt that this song reflected our bond and that I needed to have the confidence that I would be with her in this life and in heaven. When someone who is alive brings up death, you immediately shrug it off and say "stop it," "shut up" or "oh, please." She asked me if she ever were to pass, that this song is played at her funeral to symbolize our bond. Little did I know, this would be the only wish I knew that Chloe would want for her end of life only two short weeks later.

Many of the signs that I am sharing with you will be weaved into more than one part of this story. Especially this song.

Chapter Four

CHLOE'S viewing was held on a Thursday evening, in preparation to then have her celebration of life service the next day. I could not get over the fact that I had to put on a dress and makeup to go see my sister's dead body for the last time. The only reference point I had was my late grandfather's open casket funeral in Alabama, which scared the shit out of me.

Immediate family was given time alone with Chloe prior to letting guests come in and see her. My mother, father, and I held sweaty hands and walked in together. I instantly lunged forward with the instinct to hug her, hold her, caress her cheek (she got all the good complexion genes), feel her soft hair, rub her hands that were crossed at her waist so delicately. This was not my sister...her cheeks and neck were swollen after being submerged in the water for hours. Her lip crease did not create the same smile. Her skin housed a different hue. This was the first time that I believed that Chloe was no longer there. The body that I was staring at was merely a shell. I realized that what had made me love my sister was not what I was staring at in the casket, it was her soul. Now that her soul was gone, her body looked like a different person, a stranger. I knew that I did not want to hold on to the image of this stranger in front of me, so I began to instantly embrace her spiritual form.

Chloe's "Celebration of Life," service, held the next day, was astounding. Hundreds of people shuffled in, there were not enough chairs in the entire venue to offer the guests. People stood outside of the doors for hours, even if they couldn't see, but to press their ears against the wall to hear the testimonies to her life and the music that lifted her memory. Strangers came forth and shared stories about how Chloe impacted, and even changed their lives. I had no idea my sister was helping so many people behind the scenes, in between when I would see her pull up in the driveway and see her rush to change for work and leave once again. It was apparent that this was no average lifetime lived. Chloe fit a lifetime of interpersonal relations, impressionable moments, and memories into twenty-one short years. Did she ever have an inkling that she was going to be different? Special? Die young?

Chapter Five

I believe that most humans, if open to them, have spiritual gifts. Maybe a strong intuition, maybe art, music, seeing the supernatural. Mine is dreams; these are the medium in which Chloe knew how to reach me. Even as a young child, I would have deja-vu' sensations where I wouldn't necessarily feel like I had been somewhere before, but had dreamt of something before that I was currently living. A 20-30 second snap shot while walking through life was all it took to make me realize that I had dreamt the exact things I was seeing. Down to what I was focusing on, what noises were around me, and who else was there with me. It is almost as though my dreams had a forward thinking component, "psychic," if you will. But most importantly, they gave me an affirmative sense that I was right where I was supposed to be, reaching the next clue on the map. Winning at the "Amazing Race," of life.

My first dream came to me while staying in my mother's house in Orlando, just shortly after the service. I must back up and mention that during the appointment where we chose Chloe's casket and urn, we also chose individual necklaces that would hold a small portion of Chloe's ashes to hold close to our chests and hearts. My mother picked a heart, my father a cross, and me a silver circle that I hoped would signify a never ending bond between Chloe and I, across life and death. My dream began with Chloe swooping in through the kitchen, and picking me up and spinning me around while hugging me (despite being my little sister, she was more "hearty" and stronger than I, making me feel physically like the little one all the time). This was something that we did often in real life. In that moment, it was not a dream...I felt the way her body wrapped around mine like it always did, even the way she moved and balanced herself, her gait pattern. She then took my hand and interlaced her fingers with mine and rubbed them, as she would always jokingly tell me "you have the softest in-betweens ever!" I saw her nail beds, each wrinkle in each joint of her fingers. I saw it, I felt it, I smelled her, it was so real. Then, being the prankster that she is, she went behind the dream version of my mom and looked back at me, winking, and saying "Watch this." She made small tickling motions towards my mom and disappeared each time my mother looked back after feeling this sensation. I was watching my spiritual sister play a joke on my mom, and begin to show me how she was going to interact with us, now that she is in a different form. Most importantly, my sister walked up to me, pressed my silver circle necklace with her ashes in it, against my chest and whispered, "I love that you have this."

She then began to tell me slightly how things worked on the other side. Chloe told me that she wasn't able to come back to visit all the time, but it is easier to do as long as we are thinking of her, remembering her, and accepting her signs. She continued to expand that each person would get different signs. My mother would receive white moths, me brown moths, and her dog, "Kyro," (which is now my pride and joy) would receive black and yellow butterflies.

After this dream, I woke up at 4 am in tears. I frantically reached for my phone to call and tell someone. My cousin, Julie, came to mind, as I knew she was accepting of spiritual gifts. Ironically, something in Julie's apartment had come falling down off of her bedside table, abruptly awakening her the exact moment that my phone call came through. Coincidence? I think not.

This would be slightly anticlimactic if I just told you that a dream is a dream, but when a dream fabricates into your real life, you know there's more to wrap your head around.

After Chloe's service, my cousins and I spent the night together to support one another. We decided to try and choose an activity that might lift our spirits and make us smile. We decided to play charades. It wasn't ten minutes into the game in which a moth came flying in with such vivacity and landed on my thigh. Everyone stopped in their tracks and stiffened because they knew about my dream. I slowly guided my hand down towards where the moth (a brown one, "my gift") had landed, and without hesitation, this animated creature crawled right in between the crease of my palm and ring finger...my soft "in-betweens". I sobbed uncontrollably. Some of my cousins laughed, stating, "Chloe could not stay away from a good time laughing with the family." It is going to sound tremendously strange calling a moth "she," but she stayed in my hand for hours, cuddled in this same spot, and I wouldn't give her up until the night got late and it would be dangerous to keep the moth in an unnatural environment. I forced it onto a leaf before falling asleep, and I forever knew that Chloe would find a way to be with me...always.

To this day, my mom feels my sister tickling her or

pinching her on a frequent basis. To this day, my mom gets heaps of white moths. To this day, I get brown moths galore... and if I am crying, one will make its way into my home in very obvious places to soothe me...

Why moths? Our best guess is that because Chloe was studying to be a vet tech, and had a strong urge for all animals, she refused to allow anyone to injure or kill a bug. Chloe would state, "guardian angels come in all shapes and sizes!" I think she was on a mission to prove this with her legacy. Upon researching the animal symbolism of the moth, it was eerie to see how parallel the life lived between Chloe and a moth truly was. Moths are vigilant in following their path of light. First and foremost, moths follow the lunar light, but when the moon is out of sight, they are lead towards man made light, which often leads to their death. I know Chloe was following a life-path lit by something bigger than us. Otherwise, she would not have been used as a sacrifice to save so many others with the law that was soon-after named in her honor. "Chloe's Law," in Florida now protects drivers from drowning by placing more guardrails around bodies of water where fatal drownings have occurred in the last ten years. It was a purpose lit by a creator, that had a man-made component of the car and a need for guardrails. Maybe this is why she sends the moth, so throw out the moth balls and embrace the unremarkable!

Chloe had never warned us about the significance of the black moths she would send, but the correlation was unmistakable when my mother woke up to an abnormally large, black moth, the day we received the tragic news that Chloe's friend had passed away in a car accident in Orlando. This was almost exactly one year since Chloe's accident in Orlando. She took one look at the moth and had a pit in her stomach, knowing something was wrong. Additionally, when my father was placed under hospice care after receiving a terminal cancer diagnosis, another black moth showed up on the awning over my front door, and we began preparing ourselves for another loss. This was almost two years after Chloe's passing.

Chapter Six

MY next dream that came from my spiritual sister was shortly after I had decided to take Kyro into my home, as my own pet. My dream began with Chloe, my mom, and Chloe's best friend, Clarissa, on a boat. We were headed towards a European country when a floating dock arrived with two suitcases, one white and one black. When I bent down to open the white suit case, my deceased dog from childhood, Kodiak, jumped out. When I opened the black suitcase, Chloe's dog, Kyro, jumped out onto the boat (Kodiak's fur is white and Kyro's is black). After spending time together on deck, Chloe then proceeded to take Kodiak under her arm, stepping down onto the floating dock, and handed me the black suitcase, with a closed-eye nod that it was time to go, symbolically handing over her beloved pet. Chloe and Kodiak floated together off into the horizon of eternity.

Chloe was blessing me with the care of her dog and giving me the message that she was thankful. It also alluded to the ability to reconnect with other animals and humans that have already passed to the other side. This was so crucial to my emotional well being. For a young adult who had never had a child, it felt like I was about to adopt a child. My responsibilities doubled, my income lessened, my priorities changed, my cleanliness level in my home decreased (dog hair, dog drool, dog smell). Chloe had assured me in my slumber that this was her wish, and I will uphold it for all of time. Now, I wouldn't trade it for the world. Kyro is a living reminder of my sweet sister each day, and what a great job she did raising him.

As my spiritual awareness was heightening around me in many parts of life, Chloe began to share with me more profound lessons about her journey through the afterlife, such as her ability to share her energy to help different people in my family and people that were a part of her life. My next dream began with Chloe walking into a hotel room with music blaring, her entrance was of course coupled with dance moves, and she was beaming. My father's entire side of the family was in the hotel room waiting for her. As she arrived, my cousin, slipped to the floor. In a flash, Chloe lifted up my cousin, a grown woman, with her two hands, coming up from a deep squat and gracefully landing her on her feet. She was showing me that it was her turn to connect with and protect this specific family member. Lo and behold, Chloe did feel more distant from me in life, while she was helping my cousin, who had been admitted to a hospital with a psychiatric illness, thoughts of suicide, depression, and other worsening symptoms. This was a resounding message that although she is in differing form now, she is not omnipresent. She has to balance who hears from her and who gets her support. It seems busier "up there" than I thought.

Chapter Seven

TIME began to pass, I attended grief counseling, and my healing crawled forward slowly. I think that Chloe could see I was progressing past my depressive state and was beginning to see that happiness would eventually be an option, therefore; in the following dream, Chloe prepped me for even more distance. Chloe was metaphorically holding my hand through the grieving process, and giving me advice along the way.

It began with Chloe and I sitting Indian-style on a carpeted floor in a hallway, facing each other. We were close but had a thick layer of plexiglass between us, where I could not hear her voice. We put our palms up to the glass and lined up our fingers, knowing that if we could touch each other we would. There was a big, blue, button on the floor, almost like the "Easy" buttons in the Staples commercials. It said, "If I could be there, I would." She made sure I read it, then deliberately pushed the button, leaving her hand pressed for minutes at a time, staring at me through the glass. This message confirmed with me that there was a higher purpose, a higher plan, a higher puppeteer that created her timeline. She didn't have control over leaving, nor coming back, but she was at peace with it.

As the process of Chloe's death moved forward, the next step on the "next of kin," to- do list was navigating the car insurance company in order to inspect and gather the rest of her belongings from the car. Chloe's cell phone had yet to turn up, and we were certain it had been in the car with her. Since murky, retention pond water flooded inches of her floorboard, employees of the insurance agencies were unable to reach into the water to check for belongings due to the liability of injury; it was then up to the family members. My mother and Chloe's closest friend, Clarissa, had no hesitation in sliding on gloves and getting on their hands and knees to frantically search for an answer.

Miraculously, the one item that remained dry in a completely submerged car was the origami bunny that I brought her back from Japan. A Japanese woman gave it to me and told me it would be my traveling buddy. I always called Chloe, "my little buddy." So I sent her pictures of the origami with me in different parts of Japan and told her my buddy was traveling with me after all. She kept it in between her cell phone and a cell phone case. It stayed dry. I cried when it entered my hands. It will always and forever stay in my cell phone case. After attempting for weeks to crack her cell phone code, and get phone records, there was nothing that landed us to an answer of her death aside from the police investigation that ruled that Chloe had fallen asleep at the wheel.

Chapter Eight

CHLOE had a passion for animals big and small. She would rescue animals and spend her money on feeding them and taking them to the vet before she could pay her own rent some months. She ended up studying to be a vet tech, on her way to being a vet for elephants as an end goal. Can you guess what sign has flooded my life since her passing? ELEPHANTS. Everywhere! Lone elephants, herds of elephants, elephants playing, elephants eating, strong elephants, playful elephants, they are absolutely everywhere, and I love every second of it. It wasn't until we began to go through Chloe's belongings that we truly realized her fervor for them. Elephant necklaces, earrings, accessories, and shirts, filled her closet.

Once I began to travel away from my home environment, I realized elephants were landing in my path, even when I wasn't around Chloe's belongings. My best friend, Kailey, and I, had a trip planned to Charleston, SC, a few weeks after Chloe's accident. Some might think it an inappropriate time for a "vaca," but I needed to get away. As I drove miles away from the city of the accident, instead of leaving it all behind, more and more became illuminated. During the drive to SC, Kailey and I began throwing around ideas of a way to raise awareness of Chloe's accident and the lack of guardrails around Florida's waterways. With her experience in having planned a previous 5K run event, we thought it would be manageable to tackle if we planned one in her honor to raise money and awareness.

Although we had booked a hotel in the middle of a wetland with marshes, herons, and should have had a pair of binoculars and an Audubon Society card in our wallet to fit in, our hotel lobby was unexpectedly lavished with a jungle theme domineered with elephants. Paintings and sculptures galore. Chloe had come alongside me to Charleston, SC.

Kailey and I began exploring the new city immediately after hotel check-in. During a carriage tour, we stopped at a red light where construction workers were working on a home located on the corner next to the stop light. Through their radio, "See You Again," was playing, making my heart race. It was unbelievable how strong Chloe's presence was.

As Kailey and I were completing one of our favorite pastimes of appetizer hopping in unknown cities, we met two people along our journey that engaged us in such grounding conversation that the city was shutting down, but a late-night pizza was certainly in order. Shockingly, as we walk into their home, iron working of elephants was their hallway centerpiece. I felt a chill like no other I have experienced before, like a sound wave coming straight from another dimension, entering my soul, whispering "I'm here." It confirmed that all of the people I met, and the conversations I had during this trip, encouraging me to go forth with the 5K planning, was the right thing to do. And we did it.

Chapter Nine

KAILEY wasn't the only friend of mine that Chloe included in her spiritual outreaches. At the time, I was seeing someone that felt very heightened to Chloe's presence in my life. Moths in his house, elephants in his environments, and then there was a dream. He was awoken in the middle of the night with a dream that I was in trouble and that he needed to go to make sure I was okay. More specifically, he was looking into a crystal ball that showed me, and Chloe's favorite color of yellow, and a medium saying that he needed to go to me. Little did he know, I had been at a wedding that night where (I'll honestly admit) an open bar got the best of me...all of me. I was barely conscious by the time my friends dropped me off at my apartment when I had to work the next morning. In addition to not having my faculties, I didn't have my apartment keys, I didn't have my cell phone charger, I didn't have my purse with my work ID in it.He was awoken by the dream and he listened, which was the most important part. He arrived at my apartment just as I was being dropped off by my friends. He had an extra key to my house, so I was able to get in and take proper care of my dog, he got my cell phone charged, and had an ID to let me into the building to get to work (a brutal day of work to say the least). My sister helped me that night. Either to make sure her dog was taken care of, or I was taken care of, she was there. She was my angel that night and forever. This is not to say that I take risks knowing I have someone watching my back, but she must know I have my weaknesses.

Even the boyfriend of my best friend, who had never met Chloe in person, saw her in a dream, sitting in the backseat of his truck, smiling brightly through the rearview mirror. I often thought that her presence in those people's lives closest to me was a sign that they were a positive influence to have in my life.

The friends that assisted me in the planning on the 5K to celebrate Chloe were flooded with moths and elephants in their environments too. It was her mark, a way of saying "thank you," maybe? A way of Chloe wanting to express her gratitude for those around me that loved me and supported me.

Chapter Ten

"AND then the stars didn't seem so far away;" our tattoo that I alluded to earlier. Why this quote? Chloe and I understood that as long as we had each other, reaching for the stars would never be unobtainable." This mostly came from the bond that was formed between us when our parents were unstable. We knew we had each other, felt the same emotions towards our broken family, and would never forget the importance of it. It was then solidified when Chloe was the first non-judgmental support I had after being the cause of my own divorce early in my life. Chloe and I both returned home to the nest that year after fallen romantic relationships and spent our days encouraging each other to rebuild despite life's pitfalls.

In our teenage years, my father became very ill with cancers of sorts and a brain injury.

As his illnesses progressed after her passing, I was sitting without her by my side when my father had one of his first brain surgeries. My drive to the hospital was abundant with anger that I had to cope with this situation on my own. It wasn't but ten minutes in the waiting room before a woman passed with an oversized, elephant tote bag, and sat down next to me in the waiting room. I then knew he would make it out of surgery okay...and he did.

Chapter Eleven

I spend a lot of time in the hospital, not only because my family has implanted beacons that lead them there on a monthly basis, but because I am an Occupational Therapist that is employed at a rehabilitation hospital. I get the privilege to help patients that are battling physical and emotional states of disability, whether temporary or permanent, to return to a life that is as independent as possible for them. Part of that is training life skills inside the hospital, and when they are ready, reintegrating them into their homes or the community. It isn't hard to believe that Chloe also found her way into my workplace.

One morning, I was standing in a shared hospital room, working with a patient on one side of the curtain, when I heard a cell phone ring from the empty side of the curtain. Since it was someone's personal phone, I allowed it to ring and ring, before I realized that the ringtone was a song that Chloe had learned how to play for me on the piano, "River flows in you." On impulse, I ripped back the curtain, to see that the patient's bed had been decorated with stuffed elephants she had brought from home. It was a mid-morning pick-me-up from none other than my spiritual sister.

On several other occasions, I would bring patients back to their homes to complete safety checks and recommend medical equipment, only to find that they "just so happened" to have a passion for elephants. I'm talking large, overbearing, focal point art of elephants. And they usually had a message of why they chose that majestic animal, or how it related to a loved one of their own that was missed.

My co-workers could not believe the amount of ironic stories, and began to see for themselves, the signs that Chloe was sending; sometimes right in front of them and even THROUGH them. One co-worker had gone on an international trip where she felt as though Chloe was "following her," with the abundant amount of Elephant signs she was seeing along the roadways in murals, etc. She kept feeling Chloe's presence and asking her "What do you want from me?", "What message am I supposed to pass on?" Meanwhile, I was having a dream back home about Chloe and Linda's late-husband being together in Heaven. Linda also felt as though Chloe was pushing her towards using her talent of quilt-making, paired with including elephants in the patterns, to eventually be successful and more than just a hobby.

Another co-worker, Kristen, always spoke to me about Chloe and wanted to learn more about her character. As she did, she began getting moths on her computer and in her yoga studio classes, which she would share with me frequently to lift my mood. Chloe chose people that she knew would believe, would reflect, and would share.

Chapter Twelve

HOW many methods of symbolism can one person be allotted in the afterlife? Because I already had moths, and elephants, and felt pretty unhinged when an olive had the power to bring me to tears. When Chloe and I would have conversations like most sisters do; love, the future, marriage, babies, she always made it a point to say what baby names she liked. Particularly, she wanted to be able to nickname my future baby, "Baby Olive." She didn't care where it was derived from…Olivia, Oliver, or just plain Olive. Chloe was ruthless about this name, and I still have no idea why.

When dragging up my apartment staircase after work one day, I noticed a green olive sitting on the first step above the ground. It sparked a happy memory of Chloe, but at that moment, that is all it concluded to. When leaving my apartment the next morning, I saw it again. Although I couldn't kick it off (despite my OCD tendencies), I figured someone would that wasn't paying attention. The olive stayed for 8 days...despite busy foot traffic and maintenance/cleaning crews. On the ninth day, it was gone. I figured all good things must end until I was walking Kyro and he hauled me over to a young woman and her dog. She was quick to introduce herself, as she was new in the complex, and stated: "this is my dog, Olive, we should get the dogs together to play sometime." No wonder she never texted me for the doggy date, as I was standing there with my mouth in a gaping hole as if she told me the winning lotto numbers. An olive, Chloe? This is weird.

It gets weirder...the next day I receive a text message from an old friend from the DC area, that I had not connected with in 2 years since my divorce, as she was a mutual friend of my ex-husband. She decided to inform me out of the blue, unsure if the message was even going to my current cell phone number, that she and her husband were blessed with a baby girl, and drumroll please...they named her Olive.

My analysis of this message was not derived from a

dream, but my own intuition. After approximately 6 months of living without Chloe, I would talk to her and tell her how scared I was that I would forget our memories together. That I would eventually run out of pictures to see. That as time went on and my memories did not include her, that all I would have is her name. I place confidence in the fact that Chloe was using this olive as a way to channel our past conversations and past aspirations together. She is helping me keep the memories alive. Just as the song, "See You Again," states…"Let the light guide your way, hold every memory as you go."

Chapter Thirteen

CHLOE'S birthday still belonged to her, in life and in death. It was important to my family that we still made that clear. I traveled to Nicaragua, where my mother is currently residing, and visited her, along with Clarissa, to make sure we were together on a day that was uncertain of what to expect and what to feel. As a mother, I can't imagine how you wouldn't relive the day Chloe was born, the true meaning of a birthday. For me, it was knowing she would have been 22 years old, and what that might have looked like for her in life, would she be finishing up her vet tech program? Moving onto a higher level of education? Still with the same boyfriend? She would have been 22 and I would be 26. The four-year difference was harsh when we were younger, but it grew sweet as we both approached adulthood.

Nicaraguan culture does not look at animals the same way we tend to in the United States. Dogs do not share a bed, let alone a couch, with humans. Cats roam, chickens are purely food. However; we were able to locate a horse ranch that valued the experience of seeing the lands of Nicaragua from horseback. As we were riding on our domesticated horses, we outlined the perimeter of a horse pasture that had more wild-seeming horses. There was one, a white horse, almost incandescent for being a wild horse that lived outside in the dirt and grass, that cantered around the perimeter. It kept stride with the horses that my mom, Clarissa, and I were riding. Our tour guide noticed this, stating, "that is the only white horse out in the pasture, it's a young one, it runs to try and find it's family...it must sense something in you."

We all shot each other insightful looks, knowing that was an encrypted message from Chloe, acknowledging the effort it took to all be together on this special day, traveling from another country. I feel as though I must defend once more, that the point of me telling my story, is to get people to truly open their eyes and minds, in order to connect or reconnect with a loved one that has passed. Is it strange to think that Chloe used a horse, and our tour guide, as a medium for portraying her message? Sure. But when you are the one feeling it, when your hair stands up in the most comforting way possible, when your eyes well up in the most beautiful way possible, when you feel for a second that you are hovering somewhere between earth and heaven being able to receive messages, is it strange? No. It's magnanimous.

I think back even to those who ruled this earth before us, Native Americans if you will, who so strongly believed in the spirit of certain animals and what they represent. They would wear the feathers, the skins, of certain animals that empowered them. They believed that animals signified certain traits in their dream life. Have we lost that mental flexibility? To think that we could get a message through an animal, originating from human spirit? Have we resorted to thinking that animals are only good for producing eggs, meat, leather purses, and a companion to teach tricks to? Chloe taught me otherwise. She taught me to see and receive the impossible, even from the inanimate, and the overlooked. For that, I am so thankful, because my world is so much brighter.

For those readers who thought that last passage was

far-fetched, at least hear me out on these next two stories. No animals involved, cross my heart.

Chapter Fourteen

IT was unfeasible to travel back to Nicaragua when Chloe's one-year "end-of-life," anniversary was approaching. Instead, Clarissa and I met up in Baltimore, MD to honor that day the best we could. In anticipating this day, it was different for me compared to the first birthday, because I felt as though I relived the scene over and over. I couldn't get the news video clips out of my head of the tow truck pulling her submerged car out of the water with her still in it, blurred out by a small square that followed her across the TV screen. I couldn't stop feeling the shock of when I was at work on a Sunday and got the first call that Chloe had died. I couldn't stop remembering me on my knees in my apartment, sobbing, mostly from shock, rather than logic. So I prayed, I prayed hard, that there would be a positive outcome from this day that we were choosing to celebrate. Because we could have ignored it...like many do. But it wasn't healthy.

Clarissa and I went on a hike, to be among nature, and brought some flower petals with us, that we had our hearts set on spreading into the water. We hiked and hiked until we located a map that showed that the only body of water was currently closed off to the public, awaiting reconstruction of certain areas. Something pulled us towards this place, so we decided, in a juvenile fashion, that we would rush in, throw the petals, and rush back out so as not to be caught breaking the rules on such an important day and shame Chloe. On the contrary, we got down to the water, spread our petals, and sat down on a picnic table because we sensed absolutely no one around the area.

I was sitting with the table to my back, and the water to my front, when I turned my trunk around in a panic to see Clarissa crying hysterically. My initial thoughts were that she was just reacting to the general emotions of the day, until she said, "Lauren, turn around." I aligned my body so my legs were underneath the picnic table, and in freshly engraved letters, it said, "CHLOE".

What are the chances? That the one place on this map that we chose to sneak into, would have my sister's name carved into the table we chose to sit at, on the day of her anniversary? It's not a chance. It's Chloe, once again, speaking to us, in multiple languages.

There was the largest, warmest, gust of wind, and we spent our time running our fingers over each letter, crying happy tears. We were right where we were meant to be. And we stayed as long as we could, without getting caught!

Chapter Fifteen

AS I trudged forward into the second year of life without my sister, I had countless encounters with dreams, moths, elephants, and olives, that even my close friends and family could vouch for. I figured my symbols had expired, that to expect something new was just plain selfish, so I savored every bit I could get. It wasn't until two years after Chloe passing, that I realized the shear strength in her ability to manipulate yet again, a different kind of message, to get through to us here on Earth.

It had taken the full two years to get a unanimous vote among the family that we were ready to spread Chloe's ashes. For me, it was such a freeing decision to make, as it battered me inside each time I looked up to the top of my closet and saw a cardboard box, with a plastic bag inside of it, holding Chloe's remains. My sister was not to stay shoved in a dark corner of a closet for the rest of my lifetime, she needed to be released. Those of us participating in this also needed a release, mentally and emotionally.

We decided that going back to the place where we had the most joyful memories of Chloe's childhood was the place to be, which required leaving Florida and flying to Maryland. My mother found a way to rent an electric boat that did not require a boating license. As horrifying as that sounds, it gave us the opportunity to be only among those that loved Chloe, no strangers to engage with on the boat. Before pushing us off the dock, the business owner showed us on a map some serene places to go outside of the main boat traffic, my mother happened to ask "Does this connect to the Severn River at all?" This was the waterway closest to the house we lived in during our childhood. The owner stated that with the slow speed on this boat, and the limited time frame of two hours, it would be impossible to safely navigate there and back.

We were only 25 minutes into cruising before we realized we had absolutely no idea how to identify where we were on the map. The map seemed like an aerial "Google

Earth" shot from space, with a few red buoys marked. It was decided that we would eliminate the stress of being navigators and leave it up to intuition to find a good place.

The anxiety among us begin to rise once again as we realized we had only 40 minutes before the boat was due back to the dock, and we had yet to find a special spot. From all the way across the river, we spotted what could have been a canal, or at least a nook to get away from the other big boats. We cut through waves with a whopping 6 mph to get to our nook...it was perfect and gorgeous. The water was calm, the plants around the bank had blooms, the sky was clear, and it was just us. It felt like we were the only ones on the water for those few minutes.

As we played songs that reminded us of Chloe, "See You Again," and "River Flows in You," being some of them, one by one, we let the ashes run out of the bag, through our fingers, and back to nature. We cried, we smiled, we hugged. As we were about to gather ourselves to head back, one boat passed by us, with a boat name written largely on its side, "Carry On," its passengers waving encouragingly.

The owners of that boat had no idea that they were a part of a larger plan to deliver a message to us, just by crossing our path at that exact moment. Chloe had approved our decision to let her go and was encouraging us to keep taking steps forward.

Preparing to fly back, I found myself in an airport convenience store loading up with snacks for the plane. Despite the large crowd of travelers all coming to the same store by their gate, my ears tuned into the song that was playing over the speaker, "Carry On," by the band "FUN," declaring "...may the past be the sound of your feet upon the ground, carry on." To the store, it was probably just part of a non-partisan, family-friendly, playlist that repeated six times a day during business hours. To me, it was a green light from my sister above, that she wanted us all to move onward.

There is a last, but never a least in this story. I left the convenient store, went directly across the way to find a connected row of airport seats to sit in and eat my purchased snacks. I glanced back up to the store where I had just experienced something so moving, and I began to tear up as I saw the name of the store itself was called "Carry On." At this point, I figured maybe I was seeing things, so I checked my receipt from the register, and there it was, the business name printed in bold on top, "Carry On."

Chapter Sixteen

IN deciding to document these memories and messages in a book, I hoped to do more than just give someone goose bumps, or elicit an emotional response here and there. I wanted to admit that before my sister passed away, I was a hypocrite. I was not one to believe stories that involved the supernatural, question the afterlife, let alone engage myself in "ghostly" adventures. I questioned why certain levels of spirituality were looked at negatively by religion.

But now it's different, now it's my sister. It is not scary anymore. It may not change for you either until you lose someone close enough that you want to connect with, and that's okay. I thank you for holding on long enough to hear my story.

For those of you who feel that an open mind is in your near future, it has only brought me joy and healing. I have only gained from my new relationship with my sister, never lost. There are so many people out there who have lost loved ones that are still struggling with denial, depression, guilt, and darkness. Having an open mind towards allowing your loved one to connect with you spiritually could truly repair some of these things.

Talk to your loved ones, (whether it is out loud or in your head), invite them into your dreams, thank them when you do get a sign or a message. Believe in fate rather than coincidence, and always trust that tingly feeling in your gut when something happens that is just a little bit "out of this world."

I may have lost my physical sibling, but I am eternally grateful for my spiritual sister.

About The Author

Lauren Walker is currently employed as an Occupational Therapist in Gainesville, FL who has had a hidden interest in creative writing since a young age. It was the inconceivable loss of Lauren's younger sister, Chloe Arenas in 2015 that triggered the use of creative writing as an opportunity to heal and regain balance in life. Lauren was also a force behind creating "Chloe's Law," a statewide FL law in 2016 requiring the use of guardrails around bodies of water where there have been fatal submerged vehicle accidents in the past 10 years.

Lauren completed her Undergraduate Degree in Health Sciences from the University of Central Florida, and her Master's Degree in Occupational Therapy from Shenandoah University, and has lived in various cities between Florida, Maryland, and Virginia along the way.

Lauren's love for leisure outside of work draws her towards physical fitness endeavors, traveling, spending time with her dog, Kyro (pictured)!

Made in the USA
Columbia, SC
05 December 2017